THE DIARY OF A BLACK RAILROAD PIONEER

JENNETTE SPENCER

DR. NES INTERNATIONAL CONSULTING & PUBLISHING

PASADENA, CA   LOS ANGELES, CA

Copyright © 2019 THE DIARY OF A BLACK RAILROAD PIONEER by JENNETTE SPENCER.
All rights reserved.

Dr. Nes International Consulting & Publishing
P.O. Box 70167
Pasadena, CA 91117
www.drnesintl.com

All rights reserved. No part of this publication may be reproduced, stored in a retrieval system, or transmitted in any form or by any means – for example, electronic, photocopy, recording – without prior written permission of the author and publisher. The only exception is brief quotations in printed reviews.

The book recounts certain events in the life of Jennette Spencer according to the author's recollection and perspective. The sole purpose of this text is intended to inform and empower the reader. All stories are retold by Spencer to her greatest recollection. Any error is solely human error. The project is not designed to defame the railroad industry, or any party or person alluded or foretold.

ISBN: 978-1-949461-04-6

Cover Photography: Jennette Spencer -railroad tracks
Cover Photography: Jennette Spencer-self-portraits
Cover Design: Jessica Land
Senior Editor: Sharp Editorial, LLC

ACKNOWLEDGMENTS

The reality of this book has given me wisdom and courage, and with wisdom and courage, I must honor my ancestors. Their presence has allowed me the education of a divine mind and a knowing that my bloodline flows with streams from many nations.

In completing this lifelong dream, I want to recognize several individuals and organizations that have contributed to the fullness of who I am.
I want to acknowledge my mother – Mrs. Willa Beatrice Scott-Spencer; my siblings – Eugene, Tangeria, Amanda, Megan, and Kedron; and my mother's brothers – Uncle Bill and Uncle Archie Scott (both having served in the United States military).

I want to thank my husband – Mr. Tyrone E. Olander – for teaching me to do business and to enjoy life. I am a stepmother to Tyrone Jr. and Kristian. Kristian married Eric Edwards, and now we have two grandchildren. They are twins, Kaleab Edwards and Elija Edwards, and I believe if we do not teach them, then there will be no future for this world.

I want to thank the schools in which I matriculated – Kenwood High School, Loop College (now called Harold Washington College), Kennedy King College, Signal School West Chicago, and Robert Morris University. I completed all phases of the aforementioned schools and have obtained several degrees because of those schools, for which I am grateful.

JENNETTE SPENCER

I want to honor the Black Employee Network (BEN) for giving me the Trailblazer Award as the first black woman signal person on the railroad which includes Chicago and Northwestern Railroad and the Union Pacific Railroad. Thank you.

I want to acknowledge the railroaders – all the engineers, train crews, section men, bridge and building workers, dispatchers, tower operators, and the Brotherhood of Railroad Signalman. We have worked together to keep each other and a plethora of passengers safe for over 35 years of my life. Thank you!

I want to especially thank the railroaders I was blessed to work with directly – Sandra (Sandy) Rainey-Tyler, Alice Eaton-Smith, Steve Regulus, Angie DeSimone, Charlie Kocian, Ron Shorter, Paul Niziolek, Jimmy Carter, William Watson, Mike Whitaker, Mike Howard, Tanya Rice, Robert Carroll, Dr. J.T. Mayberry, Renault L. Cooks, Robert Corpus, Richard Davis, Arnold R. Robinson, Larry Moore, Niecie Y. Patterson, Gloria Barton, Norm Chappelle, Yvonne M. Walker, and the hundreds of employees of the Union Pacific. I am grateful to know all of you. You all make me better.

To my spiritual advisors – Rev. Johnny Coleman, John Pitts, Denise Eligan, Rev. James Parker, Mr. and Mrs. Westly Banks, Gail Woods, Robert Wiley, Ann Mills, Michelle Dunigan, and Patricia Williams – thank you for giving me the joy of living spiritually.

I want to thank my book developer and publisher, Dr. LaTasha Nesbitt (and her company, *Dr. Nes International*), for helping me stay in the creative flow of divine ideas within my story.

I want to acknowledge everyone I have met that changed my life and the lives of others. As always, I love life and the joy of laughter. Thanks to everyone for the courage you've given me, thus motivating my life.

TABLE OF CONTENTS

INTRODUCTION 7

CHAPTER 1: TRIPLE HANDICAP 9
   REFLECTIVE QUESTIONS 32

CHAPTER 2: DERAILMENT ATTEMPTS............................... 37
   REFLECTIVE QUESTIONS 63

CHAPTER 3: NOT SO SILENT WARRIOR............................. 67
   REFLECTIVE QUESTIONS 81

CHAPTER 4: RECOVERED HOPE 85
   REFLECTIVE QUESTIONS 92

CHAPTER 5: CONSIDERING LEGACY 97
   REFLECTIVE QUESTIONS 108

PICTURE PREVIEW 113

POEM: IF YOU SEE ME...119
   BY JENNETTE SPENCER 119

CONTACT AUTHOR.. 121

JENNETTE SPENCER

Blank pages are intentional

INTRODUCTION

This memoir tells a story from someone's life rather than a story of one's life.

When I retired from the railroad industry in January 2014, following 35 years of service, I set out to complete my memoir. Though a few failed attempts, I tried again. Here, in your hands, you hold one of my victories. Many days, I sat in deep contemplation as I battled, enraged, recollected, and engaged with the embedded memories of my past as I fought back tears while hashing out some of my truths. Hence, in the next several pages, you will uncover some of my journey regarding my family and upbringing, educational and business pursuits, instances of personal trauma, and large portions of my career with railroads.

Though there are 23.5 million black women in the United States, and we have dominated with excellence in every field from business, to technology, to the sciences, there still exists a challenge to be viewed as valuable, important, and necessary. While many have attempted, not many have delivered an accurate portrayal of who we really are. Few are willing to capture the level of deep-seated grief we have carried as a result of being overlooked, underrated, undervalued, and berated. Rarely have those who are the writers of history cared enough to document or provide evidence of the power we truly possess.

Although these challenges persist, I want to couple the responsibility of sharing with the world what it means to be black and a woman. In this book, I share a part of my journey as a black woman in America within a professional arena in which we are commonly outnumbered.

In a male, white-dominated world, I was forced to find meaning in who I was and what I meant in every space. From the complex walls of my own home, to the scrutinizing corridors of my elementary and high school, to the exploratory classes in colleges, the Southside of Chicago was the place in which I found my way.

More than being enlightened about my course, I want to engage you, the reader. As you gain lessons through reading my story, each chapter is concluded with *Life-Application Reflections* and lined pages for you to answer those questions. I want you to take time to document some of your truths.

Thank you for journeying with me.

1
TRIPLE HANDICAP

Growing up African in America, female & dark-skin

I looked just like my mother. In fact, many said we could pass for twins sisters. We both had been afflicted with the triple handicap; we were African in America, female. My mother and I shared the same dark chocolate-skin and deep brown eyes. Even our hands were the same – dainty yet useful and strong. Our full, heart-shaped lips were nearly the same, yet Mother knew I had a proclivity not to bite my tongue.

In fact, many said we could pass as twins. We both had been afflicted with the triple handicap – African in America, female, and dark-skinned. Much of my life, I hated this truth. Mainly, the disgust came because nearly everyone – the kids in my kindergarten class, those in my high school halls, some I encountered in the street, and deep trickles that echoed in my places of work – consistently reminded me of the ugliness that surrounded this truth. Often, they never took the time to get to know me, but their hearts filled with hate at the sight of encountering my presence.

African in America.
Girl.
Dark-skin.

Some of the injustices that represent the former descriptors are generally understood, many of which will be explored later in my story, but the latter is where I want to spend some time.

Pictured: 1 Me and mother outside. I was approximately six months old.

I was born in the scorching hot cotton fields of Mississippi, on the 7th day of January in 1954. However, the hatred of my kind stemmed long before me. In the early 1900s, according to Georgetown sociology professor, Michael Eric Dyson, "New Orleans invented the brown paper bag party – usually at a gathering in a home – where anyone darker than the bag attached to the door was denied entrance." Though these practices existed within communities of color, it inherently stemmed from systems of slavery. For decades, fairer-skinned slaves were given preferential treatment when darker skin slaves were often criminalized. This notion of colorism can be witnessed in various areas today. While the privilege of light skin over dark can be seen intra-racially today, it is a significant interracial issue as well. In fact, researchers Lance Hannon, Robert DeFina, and Sarah Bruch found in their 2013 study that black female students with dark skin were three times more likely to be suspended at school than their light-skinned African American counterparts. In a 2010 New York Times article, author Shankar Vedantam suggests, "Dozens of research studies have shown that skin tone and other racial features play powerful roles in who gets ahead and who does not. These factors regularly determine who gets hired, who gets convicted, and who gets elected."

I remember one particular day in the summer of 1978 when I jumped in my car and drove to the store to get a pack of cigarettes. That day remains in a deep corner of my mind because I was yet again reminded that I was African in America, no longer a girl, now a woman, and still dark-skinned.

I ran down the stairs and jumped in my yellow Pinto. I drove to 53rd Street, just past the viaduct. There was a pizza place on the right side of the street and a liquor store to the left. I will never forget that day. I was going to get some cigarettes, but I was carjacked and raped at gunpoint. He had me for hours. He pulled me from the car as I kicked and screamed. I fought intently as he covered my mouth and then my eyes. It seemed as if we had walked for miles, but once we stopped, he violently threw me to the ground. I believed this was only the preview before the end of my life. He began ripping my clothes and then my underwear. My fighting did not lead to victory. He forced his penis inside of me as I laid on the cold concrete just under the viaduct, I had driven under what seemed liked seconds earlier. As tears left my eyes, streamed down my face, and poured over the concrete, I could see my vehicle, my small yellow Pinto, in the blurred distance.

He had his way with me for hours that night. As he gathered my body from the concrete surface, he never really spoke a word. Neither did I. The entire course of events and fear of the unknown paralyzed my entire being.

Finally, we arrived at a location. I believe it was near 78th and Exchange. I could hear lots of people chattering outside the vehicle. Once he removed the blindfold, I could see that we were at a local bar. It was then that I began to regain the hope I had left on the concrete under that viaduct. Outwardly, I stayed the same – calm, obedient, and thinking of escape plans – yet from the moment we arrived, I was devising a plan and trying to find the answers to the questions on my mind.

How in the hell can I escape from here?
Will someone notice that I had been violated?

So, I devised a planned.

He allowed me to go into the restroom, at which point I locked myself in and came out only after I heard the music turn off and the chattering cease. I told the bartender to call the police. They never showed, yet I was able to escape. I drove myself home and then called the police. One of the officers was convinced that the rapist was my boyfriend. However, when I made it to the hospital, they performed a rape kit to confirm my story. Society has a tremendously difficult time understanding the validity of black women as victims.

Despite these truths, as I grew, I attempted to manage my significance. From my beginnings, my family life forced me to become an astute manager; a manager is one who controls and manipulates resources and expenditures, as of a household. My resources, however, were more internal than external. This internal drive soon impacted my lack of experiences inside and outside my home environment.

Family Life

On January 7, 1954, the temperature was around 84 degrees with a heat index of about 95. My mother stood bursting at the seams as the intensity of the sun in a blazing hot field in Sunflower, Mississippi, nearly scorched her back. She struggled as she tried to balance completing her job of picking bushels of cotton and laboring to deliver me. Eventually, she hurled the satchel towards her midwife, Jennette, who hurriedly rushed to my mom's aid. Her midwife, Jennette, was said to be a beautifully spirited woman. She and my mother were credited in ushering my presence into the world.

As you have probably already guessed, my mom named me after her midwife, Jennette. She was said to be very skillful in her duties, especially that day.

I was the oldest of my mother's children that survived. Mother told me that she had given birth to a son, but he did not survive at birth. I often wondered if life would have been different for me if he were here with me. I can only imagine what he would have been able to help me with such as learning and academics and even the streets.

Among her friends, my mother was considered the "Bible thumper." While she was devout in her Christian beliefs, she did not go to church, but she sent us, her children, every Sunday. Though my parents were married at the time of my birth, I have no memory of my daddy. When I got older, however, I recall Mother mentioning that he struggled with drugs of some sort. I am not certain if he is still alive. In fact, if I passed him on a street corner or in an office building, I would not recognize him as my own.

Pictured: 2 My mom and dad.

My brother, Eugene, and my sister, Tangeria, were born within a few years of me. We left Mississippi when I was three and headed to Memphis, Tennessee. Tennessee is where Eugene was born. I do not have much of a memory of Tennessee, but our time there was brief. Our final destination was Chicago, Illinois. Like the countless families who migrated to the north, we were in search of more educational, social, and economic opportunities for our family.

However, in the late 50s and early 60s, even in the north, racial discrimination and lack of acceptance by white citizens of Chicago were still present. The Spencer family migrated to the Southside of Chicago in the Great Grand Crossing neighborhood, near 71st and Eberhart, to live with our cousin, Thelma McKinney.

Soon after, I had become a big sister again. I now had a younger brother and two sisters. My brother, Eugene Spencer, was born on August 15, 1955. He could be characterized as a busybody, always finding trouble. One day, while playing at the top of the stairwell, he accidentally fell down a flight of stairs. Once we found him, his skull was cracked. He survived the accident, but the crack left him open to "special care" for the rest of his life. This care was not medicinal, but what many southern families called "spoiled." Being one of the only boys, Eugene garnered plenty of attention from my mom, other family members, and even the young ladies throughout the neighborhood. Eugene was, indeed, beloved. Unfortunately, ten years ago, Eugene died from several health complications during his adult life after being run over by a car when he moved to California.

My middle sister, Thelma Mae Spencer (also known as Tangeria), was born on January 7, 1957. We share the same birthday, but I am three years her senior.

Picture 3: Me, in glasses, (top left), my brother, Eugene, (bottom left). Behind Eugene is Thelma (center). Mother is pictured holding Amanda (right).

Amanda is my last-born sibling. She was born on July 15, 1960. Amanda's father is a native Chicagoan named Lawrence. Our situation was different but normal for the times. One of our family friends, Nellie, helped raise Amanda. When blacks suffered financially, it was culturally acceptable for others to extend themselves in that way. Plus, Nellie never gave birth to any children of her own.

Therefore, Amanda grew up in a totally different household, but one very close to our mother. In the Chicago flat, Nellie lived downstairs on the first level, and we lived upstairs.

Though Amanda and I were not initially in the same living quarters, by none of her doing, her presence reminded me of my darkness. She was of a fairer complexion. Granted, as the youngest, you are often given a pass on the responsibilities the rest of us consistently share, but there was a difference, and the difference was noticeable. Amanda had an active father in her life while Mother only allowed us to receive Holy Bibles, socks, and second-hand clothing during Christmas. Amanda's space was loaded with dolls, clothing, and dollhouses. The disparities were there, but for me, there were more important tasks in which to attend.

While Mother worked, I cared for my siblings. Tangeria would jokingly call me "Mother" because there were weeks when they saw me more than Mother. Our room had two beds, yet the room was very small, resembling the size of a closet.

Mother was a strong woman. She was illiterate, but she was also determined. Once we got to Illinois, she was adamant about completing her education. She earned her GED and went on to work faithfully at Blue Cross and Blue Shield of Illinois as a Cook.

Mom and I shared a lot together. I was her helper and firstborn. She shared with me how members of her family molested her as a kid. Hence, she shielded us from many of her relatives. While Mother never spoke in detail about what she endured, her actions were telling. Soon, Mother turned to alcohol to cope with her abuse. Some days were good; others were not.

We mostly got along, but when it was time for homework, at one point, she could no longer help me because she was illiterate. As a result, I became frustrated. One evening, it was late, and much of my homework had yet to be completed. Emotions were everywhere. So, I screamed at her. "You need to go back to school!" Although I meant what I said, I regretted those words. My mouth got me in a lot of trouble that night and many nights and days to follow. In fact, as a kid, I could not wait to learn how to cuss. It was one of the highlights of my childhood. Anytime Mother got a whiff of it, she forced me to wash my mouth out with soap.

When I was around ten years old, I cannot remember the cause, but we experienced three consecutive fires in our home. Once, after the blazes were tamed, I peered through the smoke as I watched one of the firemen eat some of our food. I felt violated and told him to stop. He quickly glared back at me, making me realize he did not respect me or our home. Mother pulled me by the arm as to say I should not disrespect authority, but it was him that was doing the disrespecting. I wondered how he could steal from a poor family.

Disturbed by this instance, I became even more protective of our home. While Mother worked, I became the manager of our two-room apartment. One room had two king-size beds in which we all shared, and the other room was the kitchen/washing area. The kitchen had a large metal tub. I hand-washed and scrubbed clothes with our washing board, and this room was where we always took our nightly baths. I was responsible for cooking meals for our family. I spent countless hours scrubbing floors, cleaning the walls, and getting my siblings ready for school each day. Once my chores were done, I spent time on my academics. I was adamant about overcoming my learning disability. I stayed after school, every day, to practice reading and learn how to spell and use the dictionary. I especially loved math and science, and I was an avid learner. When other kids were playing outside, I explored new dimensions of life through reading. Despite my learning challenges, I somehow always knew that there was something greater inside of me. I wanted more, and I felt responsible to be the one to obtain more than Mother's generation.

Oddly, school became my safe place. At school, I learned early on that being black was not a good thing. Eventually, I developed and adopted the same sentiment. I hated being black. In fact, all the children in my elementary school mocked me because of my dark skin. It hurt, but I was willing to endure it because their torment was not nearly as bad as having to be the boss at home. Though school became an adventure I welcomed, I was always in the principal's office because I wore glasses. When my classmates made fun of my glasses, I threatened to beat them up after school. I was sort of a quiet bully. I did not want the fights to interrupt my education, so I often punched them after the bell rang. School was important to me. I was only responsible for myself there. It became a place of comfort.

Pictured: 4 Nine-year-old me with my siblings and an unknown neighbor.

Pictured: 5 Me, ten years old.

Pictured: 6 Me and my siblings. I was 12 years old.

Pictured: 7 Mother and I; I was 14 years old.

During that time, I drew closer to my teachers. My teachers loved me, and they would bring me clothes and shoes. I stayed after school to get extra help. Soon, I began to excel at school and became more studious, too. Among my peers, I became known as the teacher's pet, but I did not care because I loved school. I felt free from doing all the housework, cleaning, and cooking.

Mother persisted when she could. It appeared she kept it together rather well because she never allowed any men around us. I was the only one she trusted to care for the other children. I took the responsibility quite seriously. However, because of this lofty responsibility at such a young age, I grew up rather quickly. After all, real lives depended on me.

Mother had two brothers, William and Archie Scott. Eventually, they were the only men she allowed to be with us alone. They were military men of great discipline. My Uncle Archie was in the U.S. Army and specialized in communications. He was more of a laid-back personality, a very nice and polite gentleman. He loved electronics. I was intrigued by Uncle Bill. He was the first male nurse I knew, and he spoke eight languages. When he babysat us, he tied us to a few chairs. We were never hurt by it, but he wanted to ensure we did not move. I thought he was funny, but my sister and brother were afraid of him. Uncle Bill took his responsibility of caring for us rather seriously. Once Mother got word of this, she did not allow Uncle Bill to watch us anymore. He died before I went to high school, and over 500 people attended his funeral. I was impressed by the 21-gun salute and the well-dressed military guys. His presence in my life was a strong force and influenced much of my self-discipline later in life.

Pictured: 8 Me during my junior year of high school.

I graduated from elementary school with honors and was accepted into one of the top tier high schools on the Southside of Chicago, Kenwood Academy. I entered high school and was coming of age on the heels of the assassination of key figures like Malcolm X, Martin Luther King Jr., and the Kennedy brothers. I studied the rise of the Black Panther Party. I watched all this happen on the sidelines but soon understood the bigger picture of the political climate of America. Malcolm X, MLK, and the Black Panthers were my heroes.

The atmosphere at school and home started to affect me more. My family life was still intense, and my responsibilities at home never ceased. As my siblings got older, I made sure they stayed on top of their grades, and I tried my best to keep the house in pristine shape. Mother was doing well at work. Instead of becoming depressed about my reality, I started to plan and envision my life differently. My involvement in extracurricular activities persisted. I tried my hand at the cheerleader team, pom-pom girls, and the basketball team. I sang in the premier regional choir under the renowned leadership of Ms. McFarland. We sang at the Opera House, regularly, as backup vocalists. The legendary singer, Chaka Khan, often visited because she trained with Ms. McFarland as well. The choir traveled and competed around the city and throughout the state. These activities gave me more time away from my managerial duties, as I became desperate to stay out of the house. To help with my financial needs, I started looking for a job. I wanted to get the latest clothing styles that graced the halls of my high school corridors in the early 70s. My first job was at the age of 16. I served as a camp monitor at the Chicago Park District. I was somehow able to juggle multiple jobs. Later, I worked part-time at the historical *Ribs-N-Bibs* restaurant and as a babysitter for Mrs.

Roberson's children during the weekends. Other jobs I had were working as a cashier at Woolworth and waitressing at a restaurant named Moon, which was also located in the Hyde Park neighborhood.

After work, when I would come home with money, Eugene and Tangeria would take turn robbing me as I slept. For a while, I didn't realize what was happening. However, one day, I waited and caught them. After work, I showered and set the house for the next day. Instead of going directly to bed, I fake slept. Just as I turned over, they pounced on my hard-earned money. That night, I caught them in the act. I wanted them to know that I knew what they were doing, and they were shocked that I caught them.

By my senior year, I was heavily on the dating scene. It was all new for me. My three jobs enabled me to take better care of my appearance, and boys started to take notice. I met a boy named Robert at a basketball game, and soon after that, we started to get serious. I was then introduced to sex for the first time. This ended in pregnant. Needless to say, Mother was disappointed. Sadly, I got an abortion without her knowledge.

After enduring the trauma of an abortion, I felt the need to keep myself up, at least on the outside. I loved nice clothes. My first large purchase was from an upscale boutique in

Hyde Park, a $300 orange chiffon prom dress. My niece now owns the exact dress and wore it to her prom. The crazy thing is, I never got to actually go to prom. You see, my prom date stood me up. He had become infuriated about the abortion. I had given him an ultimatum – we get married, or I go through with the abortion. Well, he never showed that night.

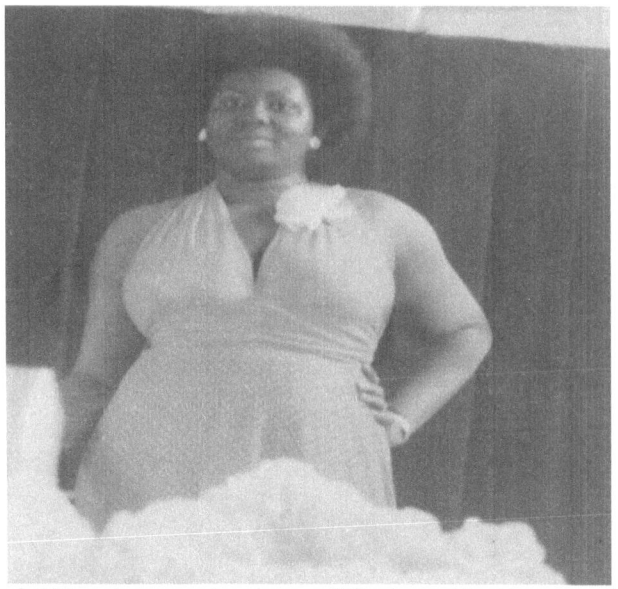

Pictured: 9 Me and my prom dress (orange chiffon dress with white small polka dots on the skirt area).

Heartbroken, I pressed forward the only way I could, still working often yet remaining adamant about keeping my grades in top-notch condition in hopes of attending a faraway college. Also, I remained active at school and in activities. I ran the 440-race during track season. I trained to become a lifeguard because I loved the water. To stay disciplined, I studied Judo, Karate, and Jiu-Jitsu. During off weekends, I trained under Diane Blackburn for ballet, modern, and African dance. I maintained a few friendships and was nicknamed "Giggles" as my laugh became infectious and could be heard throughout the halls of Kenwood High.

I graduated from high school in June of 1972 but could have graduated earlier. I had achieved such stature within scholarship that I could have gone to college in my sophomore year in high school and earn at least four scholarships. I had plans to become a brain surgeon. I got accepted in Iowa, Nebraska, and those small states. However, my plans and visions were short-lived. Mother would not let me go, and I hated her for it.

"If you're going to be a doctor, you can be one right here!" Mother demanded.

For years, I held on to deep-seated anger towards Mother regarding my education. I knew for sure that my ambition to be a brain surgeon would not be met if I stayed at home. I needed to understand why she wanted to keep her firstborn from achieving such an ambitious yet reachable dream. Consequently, I confronted her. We were in the kitchen one day, and I randomly shouted "why?!" Mother looked confused because she had no idea what I was referencing. A few years had passed, and I had not spoken a word of the situation.

Finally, I continued with my initial outburst. "Why couldn't I go away to school?"

Mother took a long pause and sighed. She beckoned her hand for me to sit at the antiquated table in our makeshift kitchen. Impatiently, I sat down and gazed out of the dimly lit window. Mother provided an explanation that gave me peace. She began to explain how all the schools in which I was accepted were situated in very small, largely conservative states. Understanding the political climate of our nation at the time, coupled with my flippant words and often bold, confrontational personality, Mother was afraid I would get lynched. She never wanted anything to happen to me. Mother wanted the best for me. That derailment was for my good.

Though that conversation gave me peace, I regretted not having it sooner. After high school, following Mother's decision, the abortion, and the break-up, I became depressed and rebelled often. I drank alcohol, among other things, which had become a daily habit for my on-again-off-again boyfriend and me. Drugs were the only way I knew to cope.

Life Application Reflections
Questions

1. Consider your beginnings. What part of your upbringing gave glimpses of who you would become?

2. What challenges, if any, did you overcome during your childhood?

3. Did the family dynamic of your childhood impact the family dynamic of your adulthood?

Reflections

Reflections

Reflections

JENNETTE SPENCER

2
DERAILMENT ATTEMPTS
Persistence through Pain

Derailments are objects, people, or situations that cause one to fail or become deflected from purpose. The sole intent of derailments is to reduce or delay one's chances for success or development. I had many things competing to deplete my hope. Being born into a poor family with high ambition was one; possessing a brain plagued with a learning disability was another. Engaging in premature sex and becoming with child was an almost un-survivable experience. My introduction to the drug scene was a door that jarred into my soul and system so deeply that I could hardly contain myself. By the time I made it to college, drugs and alcohol became constant companions. The bad choices I made were trying to catch up with me like a speeding train, yet I somehow remained highly functional.

Though I did not realize it then, I was blessed in a way some of my peers were not. Many of them had allowed their circumstances to consume the entirety of who they were. The lack of resources, and no true examples of what could be accomplished caused many of their goals and dreams to become a non-existent reality. Though the community I lived in was intrinsically diverse, there was a looming truth that existed for many blacks, especially black women in the seventies.

Even still, I realized that I was not unique to pain. Black women have been some of the most pain-inflicted, underrated beings in all the world. Our level of intellect and ingenuity have long been underestimated. Nurturing is beyond what we can provide. Our core is colored with perseverance, determination, and great pride.

Pictured: 10 Me at 20 years old.

I went on to attend a nearby college, *Loop College* (now Harold Washington College), directly following high school. I continued living with my mother and siblings. I kept excellence at the fore, but the majority of the time, I partied and played chess, Penuckle, and Bridge. However, I was not focused enough on graduation. I continued having a deep love for mathematics, and so I entered the *Control Data Institute*, where I was trained in Computer Repair and Electrons Theory. After earning my certification in 1976, I joined the Joint Apprenticeship Training Committee Program. From 1977 to 1979, I worked at the Local 701, in DuPage County, becoming the first black female electrician at that site. I was pioneering long before I understood the fullness of what it actually meant for me, my family, and those who would come after me.

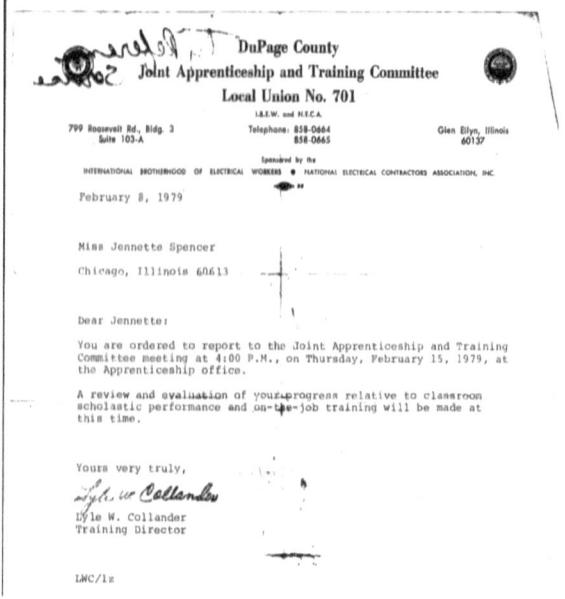

Pictured: 11 Joint Apprenticeship Program notification.

At the Local 701, I gained experience doing electrical wiring in residential and commercial properties. I learned the details on how to install switches and outlets. I also learned automobile repair. There was a lot of prejudice behavior at the plant. Once, I was called a monkey and an ape, and I was told I should return to Africa. It hurt, but I pressed forward. I worked for two years and was suddenly laid off. However, I refused to fret.

I sought out the *Urban League of Chicago*, and jobs were plentiful. One of the major legislations under President Lyndon B. Johnson's tenure was *The Civil Rights Act of 1964*. This legislation set in place affirmative action measures that allowed African Americans and traditionally marginalized groups access to places and institutions that were historically off-limits. For the first time in U.S. history, droves of black and brown students attended colleges and gained entry to places of employment they had only dreamed of. In 1979, an extension of these affirmative action measures was witnessed in the landmark case of United Steelworkers of America vs. Weber. This decision permitted employers to favor women and minorities regarding hiring decisions.

Subsequently, I applied for a new position at the *Chicago & North Western* company (C&NW), the city's oldest railroad organization. The process went smoothly. After meeting at the Urban League, I attended an interview at a building located on 500 W. Madison. I had grown to love circuitry, but I never knew I would wind up in the railroad industry. Almost immediately, I was hired as an assistant signalman in the Signal Engineering Department for C&NW.

From the onset, I tried to learn all I could about the company and my new position. In learning the history of the company, one article stated the following:

> It ran passenger cars from Kinzie and Wells streets. However, as the 20th century dawned, the Wells Street Station had become outdated and inadequate for the volume of its traffic. In addition, all trains entering or leaving C&NW's station had to cross a moveable bridge over the Chicago River's North Branch. Frequent bridge openings caused major delays to the increasingly important passenger service.

More than a decade later, in 1911, the company had relocated and built a new terminal station. By the time I made it there, the Lake Street Tower was the only one in service at the terminal. Our tower was responsible for controlling the interlocking where the station tracks joined to form a six-track throat.

My first day was strange.

It was one of my first experiences in a place where almost no one looked like me. I was quickly reminded that I was black, a woman, and dark-skin among a white, male-dominated industry. Though in a bit of shock, as I passed some of the workstations on my way to my area, some gave half-smiles and unexcited waves. Things seemed to happen in slow motion. I wanted to confront them like I normally would, but I refrained. I noticed them and yet quickly regrouped to maintain my excitement about the new endeavor. Though I was only an assistant, I knew I would be something more one day.

At the onset, everyone was assigned a meter, radio, cellphone, pager, and personal tool bag. With the crew, the environment was high intensity all the time. Going into work was a 12-hour adrenaline rush. Our job was a constantly changing jigsaw puzzle. There was always something new. Things could go from bad to worse in minutes. I got into the rhythm swiftly, as I was an eager learner.

Pictured: 12 Me on West Line tracks in 1983.

Getting used to the fast-paced pressure was not the worst of it. I walked into work, daily, knowing that most people wished I was dead. If I worked alone with one of the white guys, I was fine, but if one of their counterparts joined the team that day, things shifted. The atmosphere grew more intense. It was as if one white guy had something to prove to the other about how much he hated me.

Discrimination and humiliation were ever-present issues, especially for blacks. For instance, fellow signalmen brother,

Steve Regulus, remembered an incident that I had hoped to forget:

> "They tried to make us the laughingstock of the railroad by humiliation. They would try to make it seem that we weren't smarter than the rest of them, and most often would point out the errors that were made.
>
> In 1988 we were in the weekend crew, every little bitty little thing they would pick out, point it out and harp on it. This remember this one time, we were at HM plant, we were putting on the ... the heard that the other Maintainers on the territory were told not to go near us. We put some bonds on. We change some fogs on the plants and we put some bonds on. And at the end of the day I called the dispatcher to make sure they didn't have any circuits down or any track lights or anything like that. He told me that everything was clear. The Maintainers on the territory went out there after we left and snatched the bond off and knocked the circuit out and took it to the manager of signals. And the next Wednesday morning we were up for an investigation, and this is the way they treated us, you know?
>
> That's the truth. Ms. Spencer got time out, I got time off and this other black guy that was working with us, he got time off.
>
> ... Every weekend they would come up with something to humiliate us." I was able to realize first of all, this type racism, I always viewed it as their problem, not mine.

Until they started reaching for me, then I was forced into action. It also paid to be a hell of a lot smarter than they were. You had to be smarter than they were, but then as the same time you had to suppress that intelligence because you didn't want to know what you were about. It was just like being on stage. When the spotlight went on, you have to start doing your dance. That's when you let them know what you're about."

In the railroad industry, it was very difficult for blacks to be recognized for intelligence. We were good with our hands; so, we dug.

I worked with the signal crew. My jobs were primarily in field maintenance and required practical application. I had to dig snow for ditches during the winter and install cables as control points in various locations. Being in a male-dominated field, I did not have much competition. I was able to use my intellect as well as physical stamina to dig ditches efficiently. My electrical circuitry skills were also in high demand. I was flourishing in every way. I felt at the top of my game, until the carjacking, kidnapping, and rape situation in 1978 interrupted my life. It sucked the life from me.

I began to use again to cope with the excoriating mental and emotional pain. The bold and loquacious Jenette had changed; I had become crippled by fear. I stayed indoors for six straight months. My blinds were pulled and made room for few visitors. However, I was grateful to have counselors from the State of Illinois, as they conducted sessions from my home.

I was on a leave of absence from work, but as I became well, I went back to work. When you work with all men as I did, you eventually realize they do not care about you and your feelings. I was committed to standing tall amid my psychological and emotional turmoil. However, after several collisions across the country, the advent of mandatory drug testing in 1985 had worked against me. When I got ready to go back to work after my rape episode and being off work for six months, C&NW made me submit to a drug test.

Well, I failed.

Immediately, I thought my life was over because my work was my lifeline.

However, the company was able to pay for my treatment. This benefit was included in my health contract. Employees receive two chances, and after those two chances, you are then fired. I went into long-term treatment for 18 months prior to that. I was too proud to have someone take care of me, so I maintained my job during the time of healing. I learned a lot about addiction and it's power. For a long time, I thought I was crazy; I thought I was insane. Eventually, I felt stronger, and I made it back to work.

The first time I was rehired, I was assigned to thoughtless jobs. However, my coworkers and I turned them into fun tasks. The ostracized group accepted me and never gave me any trouble. While working at the hump yards, I was able to learn how to drive those big trucks. I managed to get hit by a railcar, too, and I'm not certain if this was accidental or on purpose. Another day, I turned over into a ditch, and I was written up for that incident and eventually banned from trucks. Any small infraction cost us five to ten days of work without pay.

There was one time when I was in a crew on the north line, and I was climbing a pole. I lost my footing. Many would have panicked, and some around me hoped I did, yet I made it fun. I choose to see the bright side of things, so I slid down the 300-foot electrical pole, like a fireman leaving the station. All the guys laughed hysterically. They had never witnessed anything like it.

Pictured: 13 Me dolled up in my daily work gear.

Another time was not so funny. I was in one of those buckets over the Des Plaines River, repairing a pole line. One of my co-workers started to shake the bucket, and I screamed. While I was a skilled swimmer, my pole hung over a great body of water, the Des Plaines River. Sometimes, I felt that people were filled with hate and anger and they all wanted to dump it on me. On this particular day, there was no argument, just a feeling that persisted in our work environment.

Even though no one wanted me around, it was difficult to fire me. I had more education than all of them. They never gave me my props, but they wanted to have me around. They would often try and blackball me. Eventually, I learned to not say anything. I often kept quiet, and whenever they needed help, I was there. I allowed them to do all kinds of stupid stuff. I knew they often thought that because I was black and a woman that I didn't know shit. That was fine. I let them think whatever they wanted because I knew the truth.

One Tuesday, we were given assignments, and the bosses sectioned us into groups. There was a loud shout near me. "I ain't working with that black woman."

The manager then intervened and said, "You have to work with her!"

Their goal was to zap me of my pride and inner strength, but they never succeeded. I would say "hello" each morning, knowing they hated me.

My story is not unique when it comes to stories of workplace microaggression. People of color have persisted in spite of the pain. I come from a legacy of survivors. I survived and learned to laugh as much as I could. I survived at any cost.

However, at the tracks, especially during the holiday season, we witnessed the remains of those that did not survive. The suicide rate increased at Thanksgiving and Christmas. A few times, we saw lifeless bodies and parts scattered on the tracks. There were no special units to remove them, but some of my crew members removed the bodies. Private lives and struggles had become public spectacles for others to see.

Shortly after returning to work, I suffered an Achilles injury that kept me from work for a full year. Thankfully, the combination of good benefits and my savings account allowed me to stay above water during this time. When I returned to work, I saw the truth of what I was living among. Hate spewed in every crevice of the place. The environment lacked respect, and the hate toward me seemingly intensified.

This time, however, the laughter did not numb the pain. My homelife coupled with work stress had collided. My drug life accelerated during the time I was off work because I was not emotionally stable to deal with a lot of emotional people. Plus, my boyfriend at the time had habits that became my own. Our house reeked of the smells of a shooting gallery, and drug paraphernalia was everywhere. To be honest, I did not like the fact that he could use, and I could not. He was coping with the aftermath of a tragic car accident. While under the influence, he drove his car into the cement wall of Oakwood Cemetery on 67th Street. Once the ambulance made it to the scene of the accident, they had to cut through the metal of the car to extract his body from the vehicle. He was wheelchair-bound for months, and I was there to nurse him back to health. After about eight months, through consistent therapy, he regained strength in his legs until he was able to walk again. This was in the late 1980s. I nursed him the best I could, considering I had sustained my own injury.

In an effort to get clean before I could go back to work, I confided in my boss about my problem. I wanted him to know what was happening to me. It became mandatory that I went through a drug rehab program. When I went back to work, everyone knew my business. My privacy had been violated, yet I did not say a word. I pulled up my big girl pants and kept pressing forward.

At the railroads, there was never a rest period that allowed you to become comfortable. Rules were constantly changing, minute by minute, due to an accident somewhere on the railroad. Every year, employees had to pass an engineering test regarding track safety. There was never a tenure process. Everyone had to retest every year. It was sort of an annual reunion for us. Hundreds of us scattered in various locations throughout 23 states, with preference given to seniority.

All my life, I hung out with the boys. In fact, I was a tomboy of sorts. What they did, I thought I could do better. Often, I did do better. During training school, I heard all kinds of jokes and suggestions. Many thought I belonged home as a homemaker or babymaker instead of an Signalmen. The more they talked, the more I fought hard to excel at my duties. Upon graduation, I received an engraved shovel with my name carved into it. As an assistant, I was required to complete a two-year training school. Eight of us had enrolled together. I was relieved to see other blacks had joined as well. However, I was still the only woman. Immediately, we all learned how rigorous our course of study would be.

Pictured: 14 Signalmen class.

I was a bit disappointed to learn that some of my colleagues had hoped for my demise. They had a bet going, anticipating I would fail Signalmen School, yet I did not falter. In fact, their doubt gave me greater hope. By 1987, I was promoted to Signal Maintainer. We had our own trucks, and our work was out in the field. We got our assignments and went ahead to conduct our work. The maintainers oversaw centralized traffic control.

Becoming a signalman required me to learn circuitry, read schematics, understand layout formulas, and read computer-generated data. When the system went down, I had to troubleshoot. I loved to troubleshoot, and I loved to fix stuff. There was always a new problem to solve. In fact, the challenge of the work mesmerized me and, at times, overshadowed the intensity of the bigotry and hatred that bled from the spirit of many I was surrounded by each day.

I did not fit in, and nobody wanted me there. So, I had to learn to shut my mouth. By the time I mastered that skill, a few years had passed. I psychoanalyzed everyone I worked around. Back in college, I was a chess master. So, in this work environment, I played my life as a chess game. I observed everyone and was deeply strategic about the moves I made. My mother always taught me to be in charge. Therefore, the ingrained nature was in me as a Signal Maintainer (in the Engineering Department).

If a signal was red, as a signal maintainer, this meant there was a broken rail, missing rail, open wire, or shorted circuit.

I would have to troubleshoot what was going on in the field. Being able to read the schematics was significant back then. The first task I needed to complete was getting a track permit and a job briefing with all who would be working with my group. Then, I needed to go upstairs and make sure they were not losing indicator signals in the interlock machine. I had to ensure they were receiving a good signal when they shifted the lever from normal to reverse. If that was okay, I went out into the field and checked motors, all the contacts to the motors, and all the contacts to the switches. Lastly, I would check the relays to ensure none had burned. If I still could not figure out the issue, I would gather the team. Though they were harsh starting out, I worked with a group of 'MacGyvers'. Our territory was very in-depth, having to learn all the different circuitries that applied to the operations of signal apparatuses. We worked together to solve safety issues. If we could not solve the issue, the supervisor would be asked to assist. Our goals were to install control points and replace switches that followed Federal Regulation Administration standards. If you did something improperly, the fine was up to $10,000 and jail time. We worked as a team to keep everyone jail-free.

Signalmen were required to bid and bump a job. One year, after I became a signalman, I bid for the job for Crew Foreman at Kedzie Plant, and I got the job. I was the foreman of a 35-man crew, half black and half white. There were also a few Mexicans and a Chinese guy we put in the north end of the plant. I was six months ahead of schedule when I got bumped by a big white guy. He called all the new hires, 'Oopa Loops'. When we were doing the south end of the Kedzie plant. We dug across eight tracks, and it so happened that I did not get out in time when the trains were moving across the track. I got buried under the track, about seven feet under the dirt. All the guys dug rapidly to get me out. We laughed.

After becoming a signalman, I then got my Federal Communication Commission (FCC) license. This intimidated most of the men. Federal licensing required me to learn over 300 mathematical formulas in order to receive my license from FCC, along with a host of other requirements. Once I completed this and my journeyman training, it allowed me to be employable as a signalman anywhere in the world.

Like always, I was committed to the task.

Imagine going to a place where everybody hated you, but they couldn't do anything about it. You had to endure the hate, but I was at a breaking point. Something needed to shift quickly, and that something was me. Before things changed, I was tested on many fronts.

In 1995, *Union Pacific Railroad* purchased C&NW. We changed our name, but many of the practices of my fellow employees remained the same.

That year, my coworker worked on Thanksgiving. He made it back about 6:30 pm that evening. He seemed tired, so I allowed him to have my office. He was a white guy. He worked hard that day and finished up ahead of time. By 9:30 p.m., I was wrapping up my work but had not heard much from him. I knocked at the office door and found him in a fetal position on the floor, dead. I checked his pulse, and it was nonexistent. His nails were blue, and I was scared. He died on my watch. I called my boss with quickness and was directed to call the ambulance and special agents. Detectives, coroners, and managers swarmed my office within an hour. There were about 30 different people there. I later learned his heart exploded in his chest. Though my shift had ended, I never left because I knew, historically, that blacks are often considered suspects. After all, I was the black woman boss with a white dead employee.

They scolded me for allowing him to relax. It was the holiday, and all our work had been completed, so I did not see an issue with this at the time.
The next day, another employee came to work and was busted for drinking on the job. These were grown men, yet

somehow, I was held liable. Many of the crews started calling me "Black Widow," insinuating that because we lost two men in two days, I was somehow responsible. There was an endless number of investigators and meetings I endured during this time. This was about three years before I retired. I was scared and humiliated.

The jokes were still on me.

One day, I walked into work, and I was the subject of discussion yet again. One of the guys actually held up my W-2. He told all the guys at the plant that I made more money than them. Once my personal information was divulged, relationships became even more strained.

Stressed mounted stress and situations were intensifying.

During a routine maintenance check at the Lake Street Plant, one of the wires sparked, causing a major electrical fire and power outage for serval months. There were round-the-clock crews working the Lake Towers, away from the Clinton Tower where the interlocking machine was, and we had to replace cables because nothing worked. We worked 24 hours anyway. There was a lot of confusion going on, but several weeks after the cable was installed, we had to troubleshoot each route. There were thousands of routes to be checked according to Federal Regulations Administration standards and railroad standards, so a lot of man hours were put into this process, and there were a lot of people telling everyone how it should be done. But remember, it had to be done safely, so it finally got done, thankfully. The entire repair process was for a sense of normality, which took over four months. It had become a dark territory.

I never stopped going to therapy, even today. During that dark period of work, I regained my courage. I returned to work, healed, changed, and recommitted. Returning to work was different than the other times because my spiritual awakening was surer than ever before. I focused on changing me instead of them. I used less profanity, too. As a leader, I wanted to connect with my employees on a more personal level. I focused on building the person instead of the employee. After a few months, they started to respond. I also implemented several annual celebratory opportunities. I used my personal money and began celebrating employee birthdays. I would bring in cakes and host private barbecues. I would bring more than 100 marinated steaks, salads, and food for all the guys in all the departments. On those days, I reported to work early to prepare the food. I called the sessions "B&B" (Building and Bonding Relationships). All the guys had lunch on me. Later, other supervisors found out about what we were doing and wanted an invitation. Rapport building became critical to my success. We did holiday cookouts and used that time to bond in a different way outside of learning new metrics.

The place that had represented deep discrimination and intense hatred was now becoming my safe place. Change started to break out in a positive way in the lives of these men.

The most gratifying thing that the black guys in the signal department did was help one of our brother signalmen complete his dream of becoming a doctor, thus earning the title of Dr. Mayberry. We suggested he work third shift at Lake Street Plant, and he accomplished his dream. He is now a doctor in Chicago, and we are all blessed to have known him.

I remained true to the excellence of my job, but I wanted to build men instead of workers. I had become a counselor and consultant of types. They began to trust me. I held sessions in my office, and the guys would come to me and talk about their problems. I knew everything about some of the guys, including hidden bank accounts where they would hide money from their wives. They knew I would never tell anyone, even though I had a reputation of running my mouth all the time.

Everything went smoothly because we communicated, and they knew I was going to be there for them no matter what happened. When I started being nice to them, this helped with my level of anger. I had to finally learn that I needed no one's approval. I had to accept their hate without becoming angry. It was a difficult plight to bear, but the quicker I learned, the more I was at peace with myself. Their hatred for me was none of my business. I finally became free of their opinions. Once I settled myself, I learned about humility. Humility meant becoming teachable. This was new to me. As a grown adult, it took some time getting there, but it happened. I went from being an extremely arrogant person to a more yielded person. I became more honest with myself, honest about the impact of the various derailments on my own life.

In continuing therapy, I went from a mental institution to a rehabilitation facility to a women's residence facility for 18 months. Then, I returned to work again, a year and a half later. I came back a different woman, a different leader. I came into the company as a fighter, and that is all I knew how to be. I began to change. I began to learn to treat them like humans instead of animals. When I changed, the environment changed, and the men changed. I went from a 35-man crew to a seven-man crew. The white men still didn't do shit I asked, but the black guys would protect me. They would say, "We got your back, Lady J!

It took decades to develop a rapport that was beneficial to me in growth and development.

In all, our crew was blessed not to suffer any physical derailments under my watch. However, due to frigid winter weather conditions, there were countless times that switches were frozen, which delayed trains. For decades, I did not like many of the people I worked with, but I loved my job. Eventually, I understood that my purpose as a pioneer was deeper than my own life and living out my purpose depended on my healthy leadership.

Pictured: 15 Me and Lake Street Crew Maintainers.

Home Life

As work-life began to settle, I focused more on healing and strategically adding relationships that would catapult me to a place of peace and spiritual prosperity. Upon going out one evening to a banquet event, I met the man I would marry, Tyrone Olander. We locked eyes, and from that moment, things shifted in each of our lives.

He was born and raised in Nassau, Bahamas, and I was a native Chicagoan. There was much for us to explore between the two of us. He loved to travel the world and engage in meaningful dialogue, and our collective interests increased. After four years, we decided to join covenant as man and wife.

Pictured: 16 Our wedding in December 8, 2002.

Despite several derailments in our lives, individually and collectively, many adventures awaited us.

Life Application Reflections
Questions

1. Do you believe derailing (as explained earlier in the text) is an inevitable part of life?

2. When was the last time you got off track (with your goals of eating better, working out, going to bed earlier, and so forth)? How did you correct it?

3. We learn from experience. Sometimes, these experiences do not have to be our own. Have you ever shared some of your derailment moments with someone from a younger generation? How did it go?

JENNETTE SPENCER

Reflections

Reflections

JENNETTE SPENCER

Reflections

3
NOT SO SILENT WARRIOR
Strategic action

From the time I was born, my mouth was something to be reckoned with. If my mom were alive, she would tell you that I was a defiant kid and my mouth got me in tons of trouble. However, for the first several years in my career life, "profane" would be an accurate description of how my language was styled. Reluctantly, I learned the power of silence.

Martin and Malcolm had deep influences on my life. My earlier fight more so resembled Malcolm. Later, Martin's influence of strategic action became a notable influence on my personality. Silence, specifically in my place of work, was an attribute I was forced to learn. However, my silence was strategically put to use. Though I remained largely silent about a lot at work, there were a few instances I had to engage higher authorities.

Once we completed our two-year training in school, we were qualified to serve in the capacity of a signalman. To provide a succinct description of what we do or did as signalmen, one site explained:

> *… Signalmen install, repair, and maintain the signal systems which railroads utilize to direct train movements. Automatic signals and switches installed and maintained by Signalmen allow railroads to move large numbers of freight and passenger trains at higher speeds and with greater safety.*

I remember most of the black signalmen performing all the digging. We almost always seemed relegated to the manual labor duty. However, many years passed before we were actually allowed to touch a wire in the bungalows or switches. Dissatisfied with our assumed incompetence, I began to observe what was happening, and then I started to learn the power of effective and precise documentation. So, I filed a grievance with the company on the part of the black signalmen that represented our plant.

I remained the only woman. I was a decade into my duties before other women started to show up in the field at our plant. There was some diversity – one white, another black, and then a Filipino. They did not stay long due to various issues. However, while they were there, I was able to assist them through some of the red tape as a result of the position. I knew my position thoroughly. In fact, when I first started at the railroad, the rulebook was so small that I could fit it in my back pocket. However, as time persisted, rules expanded. The once pocket-sized book was soon confined to briefcases. As the book grew larger, so did my knowledge. I was able to effectively defend myself with my knowledge. I was adamant about intercepting the status quo, no longer with my words, but with the written rules that the authorities had enforced.

Soon, other employees would inquire about receiving my assistance because of my official knowledge. I wrote many affidavits in support of colleagues. I used my pen instead of my mouth to navigate the darkness of discrimination and prejudice.

DATE	CASE NO.	EXPLANATION OF RECORD
10-16-79		LETTER OF REPRIMAND FOR TRUCK ACCIDENT AT PROVISO
1-19-80		LETTER OF REPRIMAND FOR VIOLATION OF RULE #23
10-30-81		DISQUALIFIED AS SIGNALMAN BY R.E. KULPA, DIV. SIG. SUPVR.
9-7-82		RETURNED TO SIGNALMANS STATUS BY LABOR RELATIONS
2-23-84		ATTENDED SAFETY CLASS RULES EXAM
3-2-83		PERSONAL INJURY. TIP OF RIGHT INDEX FINGER (NLT) PLACED ON LIGHT DUTY THROUGH MARCH 27, 1983
12-21-83		DISCIPLINE: (10 DAYS SUSPENSION ACTUAL) FAILURE TO PROTECT YOUR ASSIGNMENT ON DEC. 19, 1983. (WAIVED).
2-1-84		DISCIPLINE: (10 DAYS SUSPENSION, ACTUAL) FAILURE TO PERFORM YOUR ASSIGNMENT ON JAN. 21, 1984. (WAIVED).
6-13-84		ATTENDED CRANE SAFETY PROGRAM
1-22-85		PERSONAL RECORD REVIEWED BY R.D. BENSTON
4-10-85		ATTENDED ANNUAL RULE EXAM
		CHAIN SAW SAFETY TRAINING
		BRIDGE SAFETY TRAINING
3/10/86		Attended Pole Climbing school
4/10/86		Attended Safety Rules class
6-2-86		ATTENDED MAINTAINERS REVIEW CLASS WEST CHICAGO
3-29-88		ATTENDED SAFETY RULES EXAM
6-1-88		LEAVE OF ABSENCE ACCT. PERSONAL ILLNESS (NOT JOB RELATED)
12-??-88		RETURNED FROM LOA (RTW 12/14/88??)
9-25-89	36	LETTER OF WARNING - Job Performance

Pictured: 17 Explanation of occurrences noted.

Another time, I was asked to offer advice in a legal dispute with another major railroad company. Subsequently, the case turned out to be a success.

Recently, almost six years following retirement, I received a call from a former employee needing advice on workplace discrepancies. What was interesting about this was when I had worked with him, he never did anything I told him. I constantly had to retrain him in various areas, yet years later, he finally heeded to my instructions.

Although documentation was my forte, everything is now computerized, so the documents I once had are no longer in use. I happen to still have many documents, including the "employee miscellaneous events," which shows when I was hired on March 15, 1979. This document also shows the classes I had attended and completed, when I was injured and hired back, when I was sick, and when I was unqualified and put on medical leave. It shows all medical incidences, such as on-the-job injuries. After all, it is a rather physical job. I also held on to my examination of records which shows the disciplinary measures for all the investigations and subsequent reprimands (or, what I like to call, the reality of doing my job). In a sense, these documents tell the story of my life because there is a depth of information included in these forms. They are more than points of reference; they are a timeline of my life, accomplishments, "infractions," memories, and everything in between. Importantly, these are documents that share the truth, confirming the description and detail behind the experiences of my long-lasting career. My work with enforcing rules through documentation was a blessing and a curse. On the one hand, I gained greater respect from some of my colleagues. However, on the other hand, it prevented me from advancing in leadership within the company. The great thing was that I thoroughly enjoyed my work, so the lack of promotion was not the resounding blow that others have witnessed.

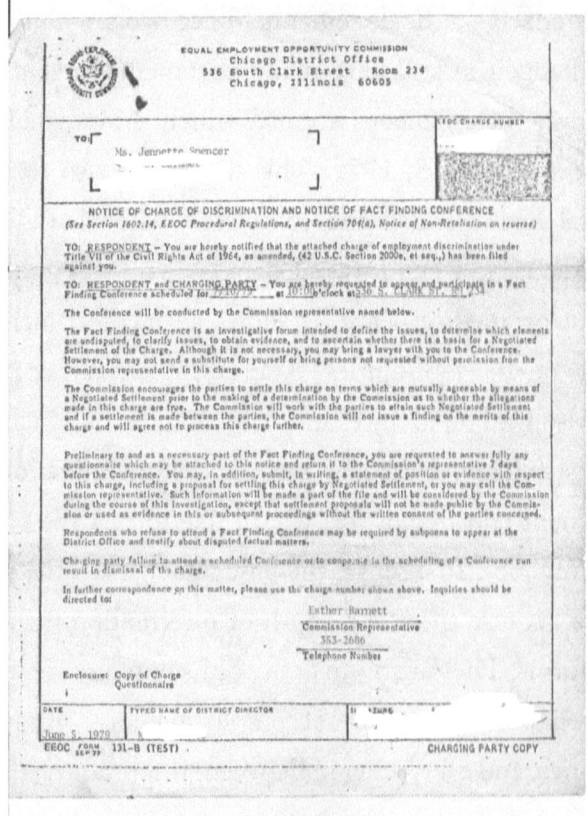

Pictured: 18 Charges against me.

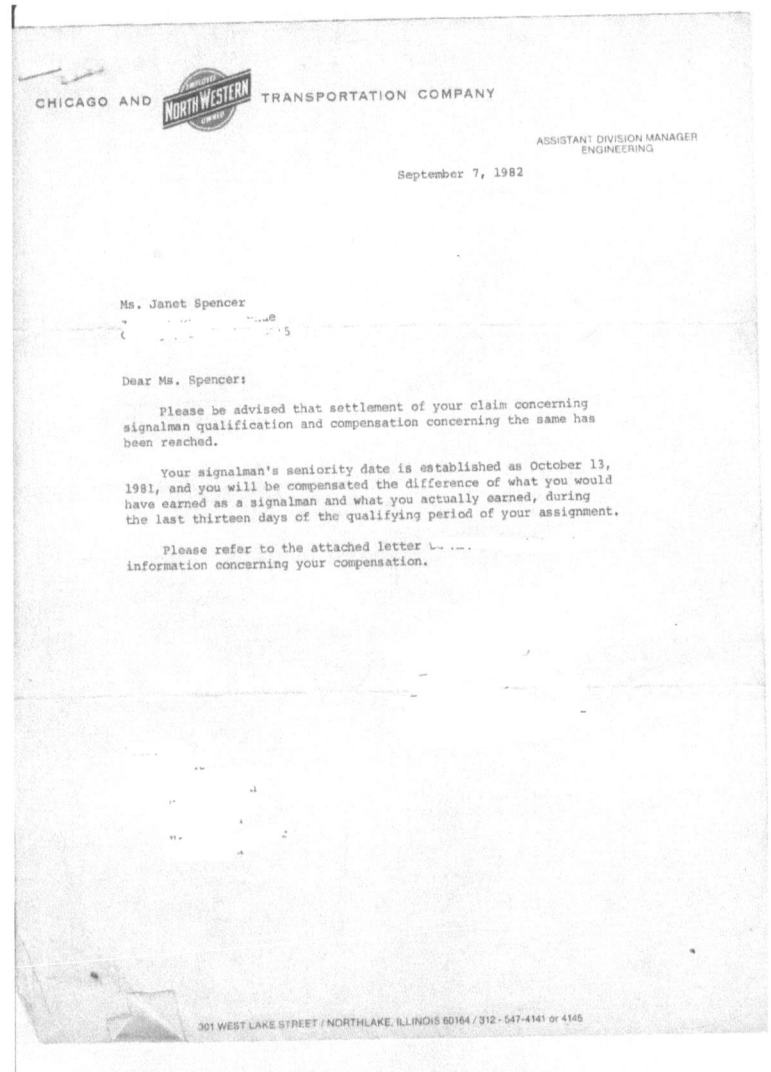

Pictured: 19 More charges against me.

Good thing, victory came, and I was vindicated in most cases. Here are some notes that I retained.

JENNETTE SPENCER

```
5-23-2001 11:45AM    FROM 312 408 2760                                P.2

                    UNION PACIFIC RAILROAD COMPANY
                              LAW DEPARTMENT
                        101 NORTH WACKER DRIVE, SUITE 1920
                             CHICAGO, ILLINOIS 60606
                              FAX NO. 312-851-8455


        May 21, 2001




        RE:  Jennette Spencer v. Union Pacific Railroad
             Company; Court No. 00 C 7445; UP Nos. 490208 and
             L-23285
```

Pictured: 20 I cannot discuss all the details but here is proof of victory.

CHICAGO and NORTH WESTERN TRANSPORTATION COMPANY

DISCIPLINE NOTICE

No: 32

                                              Office of the Assistant
Vice President -
Commuter Operations

July 14, 1992

TO: Jennette Spencer

You are hereby notified that after investigation of July 8, 1992,

"To determine your responsibility in connection with your absence from duty, without proper authority on May 28, 1992, while employed as Leader Signal Maintainer at Lake Street."

the following discipline has been applied:

NO DISCIPLINE ASSESSED

CERTIFIED MAIL NO. P462 781 800
RETURN RECEIPT REQUESTED

                                Signature:
                                Title:

RECEIPT

To:

Receipt is acknowledged of Discipline Notice No. 32 dated July 14, 1992, stating that the following discipline has been applied:

NO DISCIPLINE ASSESSED

DETACH AND   Name:
RETURN THIS RECEIPT Occupation: Leader Signal Maintainer
PROMPTLY

Pictured: 21 Another instance where truth prevailed.

Gratefully, other supportive entities like the Black Employee Network (BEN) began to champion the causes for black railroad employees at-large.

BLACK EMPLOYEE NETWORK

Founding in 1979, BEN would have a lasting impact on much of our lives. In their 2006 program:

> "The Black Employee Network (BEN) is a non-for-profit organization of black employees at Union Pacific Railroad. The organization was established in Omaha in 1979. It was conceived from the ideas of black employees during a series of luncheon meetings. The group's major concern was administration of the Company's affirmative action policies. Further, the group was concerned that black employees at Union Pacific Railroad were not being hired, promoted, recruited and retained at all levels of the Company. BEN was also established to promote scholarship and furtherance of postsecondary education among Omaha's black high school graduates. BEN was the first (and perhaps only) African-American networking organization among major U.S. railroads.
>
> Since 1979, additional BEN chapters have been established in Chicago, North Little Rock, Memphis, Kansas City, East Los Angeles, West Los Angeles, Denver, Omaha, Fort Worth, Houston, and New Orleans. Each chapter, while independent, has the same primary goals to:
>
> - Promote the applicability of the Company's affirmative action policies.
> - Promote excellence and educational scholarships.
> - Support local communities

I served as chairman for two committees: event speakers and programming. For event speakers, my primary responsibility was to book empowerment speakers for our delegation. In 2006, I booked then Senator, now President Barack Obama, as our keynote speaker. We were ecstatic about President Obama gracing the platform. However, due to unforeseen circumstances, he was unable to attend that year.

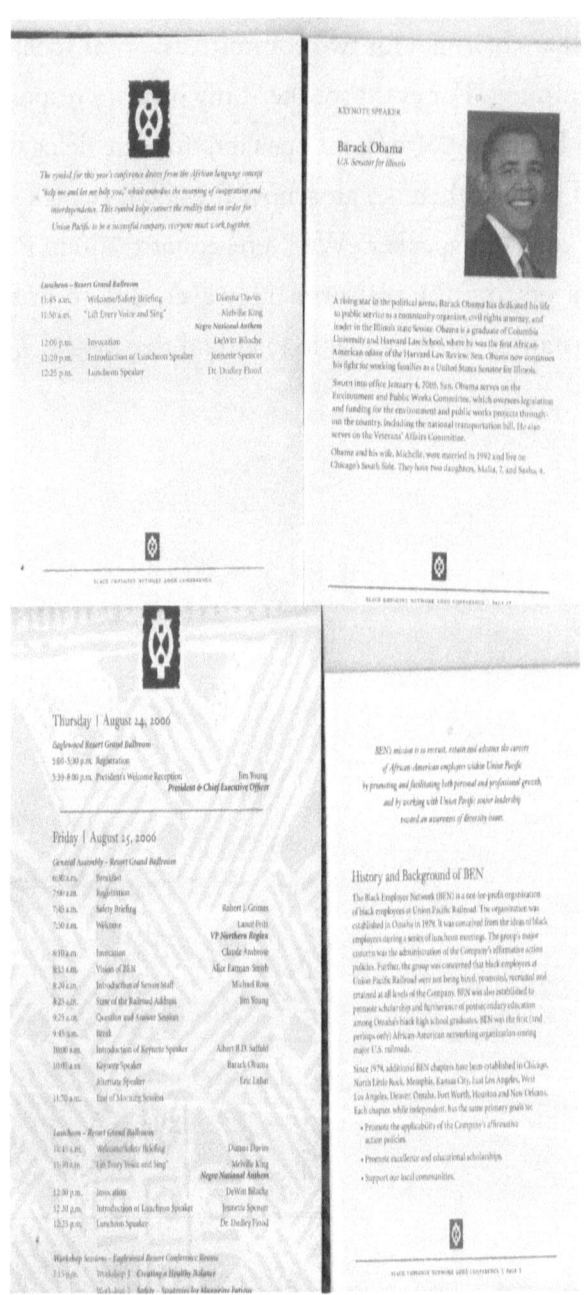

Pictured: 22 Annual BEN Conference Program in 2006.

Pictured: 23 2006 Conference Program (continued).

Pictured: 24 Yvonne M. Walker (left), Alice Eastman-Smith (center), and me (right), during one of our annual BEN conferences.

In 2011, I became treasurer of BEN's Chicago chapter. My good friend and colleague, Alice Eastman-Smith, became chapter president. We traveled extensively together, statewide and nationally. In 2012, BEN honored Alice and me with the Trailblazer Awards in our respective areas, her as president and me as a signal maintainer. In the end, our strategic silence had honored us.

Life Application Reflections
Questions

1. Describe a time in your life that you spoke out about an issue that affected you, whether a personal or business instance.

2. Identify areas in your life you are too silent and overlooked. Why do you remain silent? Why do you think you are overlooked?

3. Which communication style works best of you – conversations or writing (letters, email, or text)? Have one hard conversation today. How did it go? What could you have done differently?

JENNETTE SPENCER

Reflections

Reflections

JENNETTE SPENCER

Reflections

4

RECOVERED HOPE

More than a business

To regain my emotional and spiritual strength, I had to gain composure. Composure is a self-controlled state of mind; calmness; tranquility. We all have had to or will have to recover from something. Some recoveries are complete while others are ongoing. For me, recovery has been and continues to be a lifestyle and was once an adventurous business.

Tyrone has always been a man of great ideas. From the moment I met him, I was captivated by his ability to ideate even the simplest of tasks. Years into our union, a few brilliant ideas came to pass, one we ultimately did together. I am not certain why we choose the name Recovered, maybe because we both had experienced great hardships and were embarking on a collective life in hopes of gaining footing into the world. You see, my husband possesses a great level of business acumen. When we met, he was already a great entrepreneur. In fact, it was a role he succeeded at profusely. I, on the other hand, only knew what it meant to work on the railroads.

For me, learning entrepreneurship was tough but ultimately rewarding. When we first published in January 1998, there were few black-owned media companies. The goal of our magazine was to help those recovering from a gamut of issues. Our topics ranged from cancer, to addictions, to dealing with the aftermath of molestations, to death and grief, and you name it. With top-notch marketing, we were able to garner the support of over 5,000 consistent subscribers and were represented in stores throughout several states. Our capacity increased when we were able to interview local and well-known public figures of which included President Bill Clinton, renowned actress Della Reese, parents of sports phenomes like Deloris Jordan (mother of Michael Jordan), and Earl Woods (father of Tiger Woods).

Ultimately, before avoiding bankruptcy, we successfully published ten detailed issues of Recovered. All those issues are pictured in the next few pages.

The Diary of a Black Railroad Pioneer

JENNETTE SPENCER

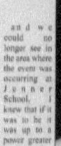

and we could no longer see in the area where the event was occurring at Jenner School. I knew that if it was to be it was up to a power greater than myself.

I seemed like time lingered as minutes seemed to be hours. However, I'll never forget the moment the Secret Service came to and told us to form a single line. They said the President would be coming down the line in a few minutes. Within minutes, the President walked into our area. For those who have never met him personally, he is most friendly and personable. He is warm and humble. And, he is very handsome. What remains of this story is my moment with the President—unedited.

PRESIDENT CLINTON: (To Reverend Demus) I saw you standing outside.

REVEREND DEMUS: This is my friend Denise.

DENISE: Hi Mr. President. My name is Denise. And this is the magazine about people going through trials and triumphs, can I ask you one question?

Denise Eligan with the President of the United States of America Bill Clinton.

PRESIDENT CLINTON: Sure.

DENISE: For all those Americans going through trials and triumphs what would you suggest to them to get over their problems, especially for those who feel like they just can't go on?

PRESIDENT CLINTON: I think it's a question of the spirit. I think people have to go deep inside and find their relationship with God and what's really important, and avoid both the highs and the lows.

DENISE: Stay centered.

PRESIDENT CLINTON: Stay centered.

DENISE: And how do you stay focused?

PRESIDENT CLINTON: I spend a lot of time reading the bible. I read a lot of other books. I talk to my wife about it a lot, and I have a small group of friends, pastors, and others with whom I speak, probably one everyday – to just work on it. To stay centered. You got to stay centered. You can never define yourself by what's happening outside of you, you got to always be at home with yourself.

DENISE: Well you're a great President. Can I just get a picture with you?

PRESIDENT CLINTON: Well, thank you. Sure.

DENISE: Can I just hold my magazine up?

PRESIDENT CLINTON: Sure.

And then, he proceeded down the line to meet others. He was real, he was genuine. And, I knew he really cared.

The End

Working on railroads, while internally rocky, represented a bit of stability as well as imprisoned me to the "norm." Working on Recovered taught me how to take great risks. Eventually, our subscriptions stopped, yet as we merged our lives, we understood that "recovered" was more than a magazine and more than an event. Recovery has been a lifestyle.

Another escapade Tyrone spearheaded was the first-ever International Tennis Tournament. In 2012, under his leadership, tennis champions from around the globe gathered in his home country of Nassau, Grand Bahamas. With thousands of onlookers, I traversed the fields with first-rate security. It was phenomenal. I could not believe in a few months times that we could pull off something so spectacular. Nonetheless, not everything with us went so well all the time. During this season of our marriage, I had become a student again. I worked nights but would attend school during the day. I stayed busy to avoid boredom. As I was coming home from school one evening, I was attacked by three men. They took me down like I was the quarterback on a football field. They duct-taped my mouth and eyes, dragged me into the hallway of my home, and opened my door, not knowing that my husband was already home. They then tackled my husband and duct-taped him in the same fashion. We laid helplessly as they emptied our place of everything we owned, room by room. We were helpless that day, but never without hope.

Hope

Shortly following retirement, I learned of many former colleagues dying due to a stroke or heart attack, some never to receive their first retirement pension. Often, the intensity of the job was so exhilaratingly exhausting that it was difficult for many to cope thereafter. Their hope had been depleted.

Through all I have experienced with my husband, I am grateful to have been able to build and maintain a genuine friendship. My husband's personable, kind, hilarious, and the life-of-the-party demeanor has made a difference in my hope. Each day as a married woman has been an adventure with him. Marriage has been the epitome of newness, as I have discovered new life. I have really enjoyed the ride. I have never had so much fun.

Pictured: 25 Tyrone and I.

Life Application Reflections

Questions

1. List some instances in which you have recovered or are still recovering. What practices have you set in place to maintain your recovery?

2. How might you use that part of your journey to assist someone else in overcoming?

3. What is your greatest hope?

Reflections

Reflections

Reflections

JENNETTE SPENCER

5
CONSIDERING LEGACY
Accepting Truth & Pressing Forward

I have fought my entire life to see the fullness of life, not to be witnessed outside of myself but to be an example, not a perfect one, of someone who truly lived. However, like many who have entered life after 40, you often question the impact of your presence.

I spent 35 years in the railroad industry, and the truth is, I was never promoted, and it took about 20 of those years to be "accepted" as an African American dark-skinned woman. For me, in the railroad industry, there existed a dichotomous relationship. On the one hand, it was a place I was never wanted, a place that was not mine. On the other hand, I eventually understood it as a place that held a part of my God-given assignment. I eventually knew that my purpose there was much bigger than myself. However, one of the things I fretted the most while being there was only existing and not living. I am not certain as to when, but I subconsciously decided the work would not kill me. At times, I turned to toxic relationships or drugs to anesthetize some of the pain I had experienced in life and at the railroad, but after deciding to break free, I was committed to living.

Mother died over 20 years ago, but growing up in that two-room apartment, I watched her pray unceasingly. I did not understand it then, but her prayer life was an act of unity, unifying with God to create a level of inner peace unhindered by others. As I learned to pray, I often asked God why He gave me such a hard life. Now, as I approach my seventh decade of life, I want to express to readers that despite some of the hands you are dealt, you are not required to inherit chaos. I have not always succeeded, but making more spiritual, meaningful, and communal connections have been at the forefront of my mind when considering my legacy.

I have maintained a great relationship with some of my colleagues from *Union Pacific Railroad*. In fact, in completing this project, I, along with my publisher, had the opportunity to speak with a couple of my colleagues, as seen in Steve's story (in Chapter Two). Steve was the only other black signal maintainer during our tenure. Steve retired one year before I did, and we were hired a few months apart.

My long-time friend and colleague, Sandy Randy, has deep roots within the railroad industry. In fact, she is a 4th-generation railroad employee. She spent 17 years in the Proviso Yard and 20 years in the engineering department downtown where we worked together. I had the pleasure of interviewing Sandy, and she shared her story with me, which is incredibly powerful and important among the narrative of my life and times as a railroad worker.

> *Including me, there were 150 years of railroad service between my family – for my grandfather, there were 30 years of service, for my uncle, 37 years, and my father, 50 years. When I retired, I was tired. I told them I couldn't go any further. So, I didn't feel like I was going to be able to do anything after that, but I've been retired for ten years now, and I thank God for that! The knock-out, drag-out part of it is rough, though. We want to do it with diplomacy.*

> *I did not come to the railroad because of my family. I was working at Sears at the time, and somebody said that the railroad is hiring, and they are paying some nice money. So, I went over there, and I got a job, never thinking of any of my family having worked for the railroad. It never crossed my mind. I just knew it was a good-paying job, and I was hired. I will never forget when I was waiting for them to review my test results. I thought, 'Well, Lord, I would like to get this job. I know it's Your Will, but I hope*

it's in Your Will that I get this job," and I did and I'm grateful. I'm grateful for my railroad tenure because it saw me through me rough years in this life.

My mother was an evangelist, a prayer. My grandfather was a praying person too, and I've always said that I worked at the railroad was unto the Lord, not unto man. And so, I worked as unto the Lord because on the railroad you might get any kind of treatment. I've had good, and I've had bad, but if you work unto the Lord, you don't worry about how they are going to act. So, that was my saving grace with the railroad.

I went into the Freight Yard when I first started there, and I quickly realized they were cutthroat with one another. I thought that, 'if they are cutthroat with one another, then I know what they got for me!" As the young people would come on, I would tell them to watch their back around here.

When I went into intermodal, I bid into the department. It was evident that they didn't want another black in there and they didn't want a woman. They were harsh! There were black men working there. The black men would cuss out some of those white guys because they wouldn't treat me right, but I had two supervisors I won't ever forget. One day, I was sitting at my desk, trying to work, and one had put his foot on the desk on one side of me, and the other put his foot on the other side of me. God got me through that because within a year, they weren't even around.

I started in Proviso, and then I came into the city. When I left intermodal, I went down to the commuter area for 20 years, and that is where I met you!

The signal department where we worked is so vital. A lot of times, you'd hear of train accidents. Well, something could have happened within that system. It's a lot to have all of that maintained and in place. With the commuter segment of the railroad, there were three different departments – engineering, mechanical, and transportation. You and I worked in engineering. I was a single parent with one son, and those years in intermodal were tiring, yet I will never forget, on more than one occasion, that you (Lady J), brought so many nice meals for the guys and us. You loved to laugh and joke, and we were all like family. Boy, those fried turkeys would go fast, but you would do that for us, and I thought that was really extraordinary. Not only that, but you didn't let the fact that they were hostile diminish who you were.

Listening to Sandy's memories, stories, and experiences about what her life was like in this male-dominated industry mirrored many of my thoughts and jogged my memory back to the realities of being a black woman in the railroad industry. Then again, there were moments of her recollections that brought a smile to my face because it felt so wonderful to connect with someone I dearly care for. As our conversation continued, Sandy graciously answered a few questions regarding her working conditions and circumstances that felt drastically different for a black woman in an industry when very few people not only didn't look like us but hardly wanted us around.

Work Conditions

Jennette: *How do you believe the racial climate change over the years?*

Sandy: *The climate was hostile. They tolerated us, but they didn't go out of their way to make sure we learned the job or kept our job. Over the years, they had a transition – losing a lot of people due to layoffs. Over time, the caliber of people changed. The white people in commuter seemed to be a better caliber than some in the freight yard. There's a ploy in these industries where they hire ignorant people to become bosses to make the work environment hostile. They don't want it to be friendly. I've heard that some of that has been happening since I retired. We worked with Union Pacific in Omaha. A lot of people who come to us come from Omaha – black people who have worked hard to have a good working reputation. Of course, the sad part is they will hire people that are prejudice to make things uncomfortable.*

Jennette: *Did conditions improve over time?*

Sandy: *No, I can't say that things got better. However, there was an increase in black leaders, but some of the environment remained tough.*

Sandy: *I rode the train to work. Over the years, while riding, I met several people. One lady had survived cancer multiple times. I was intrigued by her story. Come to find out, she had published an article in the same magazine you owned! Jennette, you were the same woman who worked in all the tough Carhart gear and steel-toe boots, but underneath all of that was an extraordinary lady!*

Pictured: 26 Sandy Randy's retirement gift that I created.

In this book, I hoped to share the possibility to persist beyond internal and external obstacles. I hoped to show you how excellence can be achieved despite missed opportunities and how my potential for success was often second-guessed. This second-guessing was not by me, but by those around me. Many of these people were white men and even some black men, yet they never had the power to keep me from my education.

Pictured: 27Graduation at 50 from Robert Morris College. Life-long learner.

Education has been the driving force that made a difference in my life's trajectory. At the age of 50, I went back to school to learn quantum psychics. As a substitute teacher, I often fret that schools are no longer developing critical thinkers. We must help children increase their vocabulary, develop their comprehension skills, and create world leaders. We must expose children to more and understand that we can never cease learning. I learned to fly airplanes at 40 years old. I still take part in competitive swim meets. I have spent time creating, too, tapping into my artistic passions and abilities. I own Spencer's Designs, a photography and graphic servicing company. I also started taking piano lessons, two years ago, to increase my knowledge of instruments. I love Beethoven, and I love studying this beautiful mode of art. As a young girl, my will to learn was insatiable, and as a woman, that same, unquenchable thirst for knowledge has yet to cease.

Here are some key essentials for living and considering my legacy concerning the legacy you are creating for yourself, because your life is valuable, you will make a difference in this world, and we need you to change the narrative of our nation and beyond:

Mistakes are inevitable.
Share love, always.
Laugh, and make others laugh, too.
Forgive swiftly.
Set and maintain boundaries.

When my friend and colleague Alice Eastman-Smith was asked about my life and legacy, she shared a depth of kind, insightful words:

Words of Alice Eastman-Smith:

> *Jennette was a stand-alone kind of person. She took a lot of ridicule being an African American women and how darker complexion and she was very vocal.*
>
> *She took pride in her job. She tried not to be aggressive. But when you are a woman and you go into a man's occupation; you are going to get harassed regardless. Truthfully, they don't want you there. But I can commend her because she stood her ground.*
> *...Her time there was a storm, and she weathered the storm of the railroad industry quite well. Having that occupation and not being wanted, she was there to stay.*
>
> *Jennette has an amazing personality. She likes to fit in, therefore, if she's with intellectual people, she wants to put on her intellectual voice. She wants to let people know: "don't look at me and sum me up because I laugh loudly.' They think*

that I'm uneducated. She has an array of gifts. She's a photographer, she's a teacher, she's signal maintainer. She's worked in a lot of fields, but her greatest field is yet to come.

I see doors opening for her, teaching not teaching what's in the book, but teaching about life.

When I consider my accomplishments, I often wonder about my parents, especially my dad. I wonder what part of him I inherited. Though I have yet to receive an opportunity to meet him, I always hoped our paths would cross. In fact, I attempted tracking him down last year but had no luck. I think I would have made him proud. Instead of becoming bitter about what I did not receive from him, I choose to welcome Mother's teachings about him and his biological legacy. Dad was Cherokee. When considering the legacy of natives, I always had it in me to become a *first*.

As you reflect on your own identity, afterwards are some pictures for your perusal. Enjoy!

Life Application Reflections
Questions

1. Identify what is important to you. List some of those things here.

2. What is your deepest regret? How can you change, release that regret, and rewrite your narrative?

3. If you died today, what legacy will you leave your family, community, and this world?

The Diary of a Black Railroad Pioneer

Reflections

Reflections

Reflections

JENNETTE SPENCER

PICTURE PREVIEW

Pictured: 28 My late brother, Eugene and Mother.

Pictured: 29 Me along with Jim Young then retired president of Union Pacific Railroad.

Pictured: 30 Me swimming in the Chicago Olympics competition.

Pictured: 31 My medals from the swim competition.

Pictured: 32 Me and my 30th year class high school reunion at Kenwood Academy.

Pictured: 33 Me flying planes at Midway Airport.

Pictured: 34 Me with community leader and radio personality, Herb Kent.

Pictured: 35 Me and businessman, investor, author, and speaker, Farrah Gray.

Pictured: 36 Me with my spiritual mentor, Yvonne M. Walker, alongside Lance Fritz (Regional Vice President-Northern Region for Union Pacific Corporation).

Pictured: 37 Tyrone, me, and Rev. Dr. Jeremiah Wright, long-time pastor of Trinity Church on Chicago's Southside.

Pictured: 38 Me, featured with a copy of the Signalmen's Journal. My photography was featured on the front cover.

Pictured: 39 The tracks that changed the route of my life. Computer operation on Lake Street plant.

The Diary of a Black Railroad Pioneer

IF YOU SEE ME

by Jennette Spencer

When you see me, you see black history.
When you see me, you see the oneness of the divine mind.
When you see me, my hair is curly, straight, or in dreadlocks.
When you see me, I have love in my heart for everyone.
When you see me, I forgive you for what has been done to my black people.
It is time to change and replace the hate in your hearts with love.
When you see me, you see truth.
When you see me, you see peace.
When you see me, I am whole.
When you see me, my eyes are dark brown and wide open.
When you see me, I am happy.
When you see me, I am laughing.
When you see me, I am free.
When you see me, I am helping others.
When you see me, I am a child of God.

JENNETTE SPENCER

CONTACT AUTHOR

Do you want to schedule a book signing or speaking event or submit confidential questions to the author? If so, please complete the contact form at www.jennettespencer.com.

Social Media:

Instagram @ JennetteSpencer
Facebook - facebook.com/jennette.spencer

DO YOU WANT TO WRITE A BOOK?
Contact our publisher at
www.drnesintl.com

www.ingramcontent.com/pod-product-compliance
Lightning Source LLC
Chambersburg PA
CBHW022143160426
43197CB00009B/1412